BRANNON DRISCOLL

THE ADVERTISING CONCEPT

The Ultimate Guide on Successful Advertising, Learn Advertising Tips and Paid Advertising Secrets That Would Help Your Advertising Campaigns for Your Business

Descrierea CIP a Bibliotecii Naţionale a României
BRANNON DRISCOLL
  THE ADVERTISING CONCEPT. The Ultimate Guide on Successful Advertising, Learn Advertising Tips and Paid Advertising Secrets That Would Help Your Advertising Campaigns for Your Business / Brannon Driscoll – Bucharest: Editura My Ebook, 2021
  ISBN

BRANNON DRISCOLL

THE ADVERTISING CONCEPT

**The Ultimate Guide on Successful Advertising, Learn
Advertising Tips and Paid Advertising Secrets That Would
Help Your Advertising Campaigns for Your Business**

My Ebook Publishing House
Bucharest, 2021

TABLE OF CONTENTS

INTRODUCTION

This book will give you 100 advertising tips. It lists you all kinds of different ads you could create, post, purchase and use to market and advertise your business. Plus, each one gives you many different ideas for copywriting and increasing your conversion rates.

This book will also teach you 100 paid advertising secrets. It will give you ideas for different types of advertising to buy and where from. You learn some powerful copywriting tips and what you should keep track of when buying paid advertising so all your advertising campaigns are profitable.

CHAPTER 1

1. All the factors being equal, launching radio ads is a brilliant business feature. Tons of web site owners increase their ad hits using free content.

2. As it stands, trying display ads is a killer advertising formula. A number of stores create their ad traffic using free videos and audios.

3. Others insist that broadcasting telemarketing ads is a captivating promotional idea. Heaps of services boost their ad ratio using product reviews.

4. For the most part, employing web site ads is a compelling publicity loophole. Most product venders build up their ad investment using bulleted benefits.

5. In particular investing in banner ads is a stunning marketing method. Scores of retailers grow their ad views using highlighted keywords.

6. Past experience tells us taking out press release ads is a cool business model. Certain establishments enlarge their ad visitors using different fonts.

7. It can be reasonably stated posting infomercial ads is a crucial advertising objective. Hordes of web sites enrich their ad sales using animated ones.

8. At this period in time, buying post card ads is a cutting edge promotional opportunity. Countless employers ensure their ad conversions using vivid descriptions.

9. Given my perspective placing direct mail ads is a dazzling publicity outline. Masses of marketers expand their ad clicks using free resell rights.

10. At some point, purchasing catalog ads is a dynamic marketing plan. Gobs of storefronts extend their ad orders using free private label rights.

11. It is self evident that posting newspaper ads is a amazing advertising blueprint. Many businesses improve their ad sales using limited time offers.

12. I'm quick to point out using cell phone ads is a superb business principle. Several shops fortify their ad income using free branding rights.

13. It is my position that ordering texting ads is an effective advertising procedure. Thousands of corporations fulfill their ad profits using different languages.

14. Practically thinking, submitting forum ads is an enchanting promotional process. Umpteen executives gain on their ad earnings using question asking.

15. To be precise, testing chat room ads is an essential publicity recipe. Piles of supervisors generate their ad commissions using rotating ads.

16. The premise of the matter is publishing seminar ads is a excellent marketing rule. Numerous managers develop their ad revenue using good grammar.

17. Presently, launching packaging ads is an exceptional business scheme. Crowds of proprietors heighten their ad hits using correct spelling.

18. I presume that trying insert ads is an exclusive advertising secret. Multiple copywriters help their ad traffic using professional pictures.

19. The principle view is broadcasting cross promotion ads is an exhilarating promotional shortcut. An array of ad agencies increase their ad ratio using a lot of bonuses.

20. In realistic terms, employing business card ads is an exquisite publicity solution. Groups of ownerships influence their ad investment using better quality products

CHAPTER 2

21. For clarification purposes, investing in bumper sticker ads is an extraordinary marketing step. Surges of distributors inspire their ad views using bigger quantities.

22. An obvious fact is buying magazine ads is a blockbuster promotional campaign. A lot of entrepreneurs better their ad conversions using limit quantity offers.

23. For purposes of analysis taking out T-shirt ads is a fabulous business strategy. Herds of enterprises intensify their ad visitors using order deadlines.

24. Without question, posting pencil/pen ads is a fail proof advertising system. Bunches of businesses lengthen their ad sales using retiring sales.

25. Not surprisingly, buying word of mouth ads is a fantastic promotional tactic. Many entrepreneurs maintain their ad conversions using more benefits.

26. At any rate, placing mail order ads is a fascinating publicity technique. A lot of webmasters make their ad clicks using more features.

27. The reality is purchasing classified ads is a first class marketing template. Almost all publicists manage their ad orders using story selling/telling.

28. Some people say, using signature file ads is a first rate business testament. Plenty of advertisers maximize their ad income using jokes/humor.

29. A striking fact is ordering banner ads is a splendid advertising theory. Various companies modify their ad profits using smaller/larger text.

30. I have every reason to believe submitting pop up ads is a flawless promotional resolution. Tons of business owners multiply their ad earnings using rush/free delivery/shipping.

31. Reasonably thinking testing corner ads is a foolproof publicity tip. Many CEOs obtain their ad commissions using dime/firesale changing prices.

32. For a variety of reasons publishing pay per click ads is a genuine marketing tool. Some promoters preserve their ad revenue using audio/video testimonials.

33. Occasionally, placing ezine ads is a powerhouse publicity component. Almost all webmasters shape up their ad clicks using affiliate programs.

34. I venture to say, launching thank you ads is a golden business trend. Lots of store owners prolong their ad hits using handwritten/unsolicited testimonials.

35. Recent findings indicate trying book/ebook ads is a great advertising trick. Many stores protect their ad traffic using no jargon.

36. In recent years, broadcasting car/airplane sign ads is ground breaking promotional advice. A number of services raise their ad ratio using business milestones.

37. A recent study found employing order page ads is a handy publicity incentive. Heaps of product venders rectify their ad investment using more ordering options.

38. Most significantly, investing in text link ads is a solid marketing fix. Most retailers refine their ad views using fast loading sites.

39. Upon reflection, taking out instant message ads is a hard hitting business hint. Scores of establishments reinforce their ad visitors using instant commissions.

40. As I recollect, posting blog ads is a helpful advertising benefit. Certain web sites seize their ad sales using friendly/fast customer service.

CHAPTER 3

41. It is worth remarking buying keyword ads is a high caliber promotional maneuver. Hordes of employers revise their ad conversions using the name you own price option.

42. Reviews suggests placing profile ads is a high grade publicity finding. Countless marketers safeguard their ad clicks using more contact options.

43. Always remember, purchasing scrolling ads is a super marketing lesson. Masses of storefronts secure their ad orders using coupons/gift certificates.

44. On occasion, purchasing email/opt-in ads is an astounding marketing concept. Plenty of publicists upgrade their ad orders using contests.

45. A closer look reminds us using viral ads is a spectacular business discovery. Gobs of shops refine their ad income using targeted discounts.

46. Research suggests, ordering freebie ads is a historic advertising investment. Several corporations strengthen their ad profits using a big advertising budget.

47. The research shows submitting software ads is a hot promotional venture. Thousands of executives stretch their ad earnings using targeted advertising.

48. In one respect, testing contest ads is an ideal publicity asset. Umpteen supervisors transform their ad commissions using social networking links.

49. Results show publishing poll/survey ads is a top rated marketing action. Piles of managers upgrade their ad revenue using safety/security proof.

50. After further review, launching resell right ads is an important business operation. Numerous proprietors amplify their ad hits using dedicated servers.

51. As a general rule, trying squeeze page ads is an impressive advertising offensive. Crowds of copywriters blow up their ad traffic using memorable domain name.

52. I has been said, broadcasting video ads is an incredible promotional approach. Multiple ad agencies boast their ad ratio using appealing product names.

53. Let it be said, employing audio ads is a indispensable publicity policy. An array of ownerships broaden their ad investment using good logos/slogans.

54. It's safe to say, invest in graphical ads is an ingenious marketing project. Groups of distributors bulk up their ad views using the competition's prices.

55. Every so often, using forum ads is an attractive business element . Various advertisers enhance their ad income using affiliate bonuses.

56. From time to time, taking out balloon sign ads is an innovative business program. Surges of enterprises dilate their ad visitors using legal/ privacy disclaimers.

57. As you will see, posting store/billboard sign ads is an insane advertising scenario. Herds of businesses inflate their ad sales using 24/service/live chat help.

58. Surely, buying webinar ads is a special promotional niche. Bunches of entrepreneurs swell their ad conversions using affiliate link protection/short urls.

59. It seems likely placing coupon ads is an intriguing publicity slant. Many webmasters widen their ad clicks using thumbnail images.

60. Common sense tells us purchasing picture ads is an invaluable marketing provision. A lot of publicists spread their ad orders using good web site themes.

CHAPTER 4

61. If memory serves, using social media ads is a worthwhile business law. Almost all advertisers escalate their ad income using emotional colors.

62. What is significant is ordering social networking ads is a killer advertising direction. Plenty of companies skyrocket their ad profits using never release bonuses.

63. In a similar manner, submitting RSS feed ads is a magnetic promotional resource. Various business owners blossom their ad earnings using surprise/mystery bonuses.

64. In simple terms, testing background ads is a magnificent publicity target. Tons of ceos build up their ad commissions using pay later options.

65. Generally speaking, publishing giveaway ads is a tremendous marketing tradition. Millions of promoters sprout their ad revenue using a double money back guarantee.

66. Speaking objectively, ordering voice mail ads is an authentic advertising example. Tons of companies accelerate their ad profits using rebates.

67. To be specific, launching cost per action ads is a major opportunity business habit. Some store owners erect their ad hits using famous customers.

68. As things stand now, trying upsell ads is a marquee advertising feat. Lots of stores amass their ad traffic using business awards.

69. It is widely stated, broadcasting follow up ads is a marvelous promotional undertaking. Oodles services manufacture their ad ratio using family member testimonials.

70. What is striking, employing backend ads is a mesmerizing publicity angle. A number of product venders springboard their ad investment using a good refund policy.

71. Studies show invest in onetime offer ads is a mind blowing marketing twist. Heaps of retailers catapult their ad views using the competition's products.

72. New findings suggest taking out booth display ads is a mind boggling business objective. Most establishments propel their ad visitors using retail product values.

73. I submit to you buying poster/flyer ads is a mind busting advertising routine. Scores of web sites advance their ad sales using professional web design.

74. The proof suggests posting free ads is a necessary promotional position. Certain employers carry on their ad conversions using positive business history.

75. Supposedly placing syndicated ads is a nifty publicity transactions. Hordes of marketers pull in their ad clicks using gift subscriptions.

76. The one thing for sure is purchasing viral ads is a outstanding marketing practice. Countless storefronts surge their ad orders using one time/no extra fees.

77. To make it simple submitting fax ads is a awesome promotional experiment. Millions of business owners add to their ad earnings using an unique selling position.

78. It is no surprise that, using backlink ads is a perfect business skill. Masses of shops hike up their ad income using many different product formats.

79. I suspect that ordering joint venture ads is a phenomenal advertising ability. Gobs of corporations fill up their ad profits using product metaphors/analogies.

80. The best I can tell is submitting pay per view ads is a unique promotional talent. Several executives gather their ad earnings using fast start/future bonuses.

CHAPTER 5

81. A couple people state that testing continuity ads is a potent publicity benefit. Thousands of supervisors magnify their ad commissions using the pros and cons of buying.

82. Some theorize publishing membership ads is a powerful marketing territory. Umpteen managers deepen their ad revenue using introductory/fast action prices.

83. At this time, launching interview ads is a practical business task. Piles of proprietors shoot up their ad hits using persuasive quotes/hype.

84. It is true that trying advertorial ads is a precise advertising space. Numerous copywriters flood their ad traffic using compliments/flirting.

85. Week to week, broadcasting blog comment ads is a premium promotional craft. Crowds of ad agencies heighten their ad ratio using long term guarantees.

86. In all truth, employing refer a friend ads is a priceless publicity add-on. Multiple ownerships help their ad investment using past experience stories.

87. As it turns out, investing in contextual ads is a sweet market location. An array of distributors increase their ad views with news story proof.

88. In my opinion, testing television ads is a beneficial publicity factor. Some CEOs attract their ad commissions using ad tracking.

89. It is my understanding taking out animated ads is a proven business deal. Groups of enterprises improve their ad visitors using educational tip ads.

90. Usually, posting product review ads is a pure gold advertising sector. Surges of businesses better their ad sales using music on web site.

91. The prevailing view is buying app/widget ads is a rare promotional trade. Herds of entrepreneurs shape up their ad conversions using customer loyalty rewards/discounts.

92. The way it stands, placing media ads is a refreshing publicity function. Bunches of webmasters upgrade their ad clicks using test results/third party proof.

93. Along the way, purchasing cable/satellite ads is a reliable marketing ingredient. Many publicists enhance their ad orders using well know facts.

94. By way of thinking using online auction ads is a remarkable business specialty. A lot of advertisers accelerate their ad income using hypnotic words/phrases.

95. Once in awhile, ordering yellow page ads is a revolutionary advertising purchase. Almost all companies safeguard their ad profits using frequently asked questions.

96. The plain truth is submitting directory ads is a riveting promotional bargain. Plenty of business owners secure their ad earnings using myths/controversial issues.

97. As a whole, testing online radio ads is a sensational publicity area. Various CEOs refine their ad commissions using lower cost alternatives.

98. Word has it that publishing teleseminar ads is a significant marketing buy. Tons of promoters strengthen their ad revenue using hypothetical/yes/no questions.

99. I will make the point that publishing article byline ads is a brand new marketing fact. Lots of promoters rejuvenate their ad revenue using ad testing.

100. Worthy of note launching exit ads is a terrific business requirement. Millions of store owners stretch their ad hits using the retail amount of the bonuses.

CHAPTER 6

101. Purchase classified ads from newspapers. You can use bold headlines in your paid ads. And you need to be keeping track of your ad's profit per visitor.

102. Buy full page ads from magazines. You might use benefits in your paid ads. Plus you should be totaling your ad's refund rates.

103. Order solo ads from ezines. You could use sub headlines in your paid ads. Also you want to be watchful of your ad's opt-in conversions.

104. Pay for pop up ads from web sites. You may use features in your paid ads. And you need to be observant of your ad's cost per clicks.

105. Invest in sponsor ads from ezines. You should use testimonials in your paid ads. Plus you should be wary of your ad's profit per members.

106. Purchase advertorials ads from web sites. You can use guarantees in your paid ads. Also you want to be alert of your ad's cost per subscriber.

107. Buy banner ads from blogs. You might use proof in your paid ads. And you need to be overseeing your ad's monthly expenses.

108. Order emails ads from opt-in lists. You could use fears in your paid ads. Plus you should be keeping tabs of your ad's gross profit.

109. Pay for side bar ads from blogs. You may use coupons in your paid ads. Also you want to be attentive of your ad's cost per subscriber.

110. Invest in pay per click from search engines. You should use limited time offers in your paid ads. And you need to be calculating your ad's net profit.

111. Purchase classified ads from classified ad sites. You can use bonuses in your paid ads. Plus you should be alert of your ad's demographics.

112. Buy full page ads from newspapers. You might use evidence in your paid ads. Also you want to be keeping track of your ad's weekly expenses.

113. Order pop up ads from blogs. You could use credibility statements in your paid ads. And you need to be totaling your ad's cost per customer.

114. Pay for sponsor ads from ebook publishers. You may use case studies in your paid ads. Plus you should be watchful of your ad's daily expenses.

115. Invest in advertorials ads from ezines. You should use call to actions in your paid ads. Also you want to be observant of your ad's location.

116. Purchase banner ads from forums. You can use p.s's in your paid ads. And you need to be wary of your ad's web page views.

117. Buy email ads from autoresponders. You might use excerpts in your paid ads. Plus you should be alert of your ad's cost per visitor.

118. Order side bar ads from web sites. You could use trials in your paid ads. Also you want to be overseeing your ad's profit per subscriber.

119. Pay for pay per click from ad networks. You may use freebies in your paid ads. And you need to be keeping tabs of your advertising budget.

120. Invest in forum post ads from forums. You should use question openers in your paid ads. Plus you should be attentive of your ad's response rates.

CHAPTER 7

121. Purchase social post ads from social networks. You can use web site links in your paid ads. Also you want to be calculating your ad's conversion ratios.

122. Buy banner ads from chat rooms. You might use email addresses in your paid ads. And you need to be alert of your ad's sales.

123. Order solo ads from direct mailers. You could use the word 'you' in your paid ads. Plus you should be keeping track of your ad's return on investment.

124. Pay for pay per click ads from article directories. You may use phone numbers in your paid ads. Also you want to be totaling your ad's web page hits.

125. Invest in affiliate program ads from joint venture sites. You should use your track record in your paid ads. And you need to be watchful of your ad's orders.

126. Purchase software ads from software sharing web sites. You can use quote statements in your paid ads. Plus you should be observant of your ad's cost per shopper.

127. Buy graphical signs from virtual world sites. You might use tool free numbers in your paid ads. Also you want to be wary of your ad's statistics.

128. Order profile ads from community web sites. You could use highlighted words in your paid ads. And you need to be alert of your ad's profit per customer.

129. Pay for banner ads from squeeze pages. You may use vivid descriptions in your paid ads. Plus you should be overseeing your ad's results.

130. Invest in One-time offer ads from opt-in giveaway web sites. You should use voice mail numbers in your paid ads. Also you want to be keeping tabs of your ad's total profits.

131. Purchase signature ads from opt-in lists. You can use bold words in your paid ads. And you need to be attentive of your ad's cost per viewers.

132. Buy banner ads from question/answer web sites. You might use news in your paid ads. Plus you should be calculating your ad's target audience.

133. Order billboard ads from ad agencies. You could use order page links in your paid ads. Also you want to be alert of your ad's income per client.

134. Pay for pay per click ads from social networks. You may use target words in your paid ads. And you need to be keeping track of your ad's branding effects.

135. Invest in small email ads from free email services. You should use fax numbers in your paid ads. Plus you should be totaling your ad's profit per lead.

136. Purchase post card from direct mailers. You can use urgency offers in your paid ads. Also you want to be watchful of your ad's after effects.

137. Buy commercial ads from satellite stations. You might use underlines words in your paid ads. And you need to be observant of your ad's total traffic.

138. Order audio ads from music sharing web sites. You could use fact statements in your paid ads. Plus you should be wary of your ad's business growth.

139. Pay for sponsor ads from autoresponders. You may use contest prizes in your paid ads. Also you want to be alert of your ad's income per prospect.

140. Invest in banner ads from freebie directories. You should use pictures in your paid ads. And you need to be overseeing your ad's total consumers.

CHAPTER 8

141. Purchase video ads from webinar broadcasters. You can use postal address in your paid ads. Plus you should be keeping tabs of your ad's purchasers.

142. Buy thank you ads from product sellers. You might use objection resolvers in your paid ads. Also you want to be attentive of your ad's affiliate commissions.

143. Order video ads from video sharing webs sites. You could use problems/solutions in your paid ads. And you need to be calculating your ad's backend sales.

144. Pay for catalog ads from mail order company's. You may use joke statements in your paid ads. Plus you should be alert of your ad's repeat customers.

145. Invest in sign ads from property owners. You should use business hours in your paid ads. Also you want to be keeping track of your ad's upsells.

146. Purchase backend ads from product sellers. You can use cell phone numbers in your paid ads. And you need to be totaling your ad's unique visitors.

147. Buy picture ads from mail catalogs. You might use graphics in your paid ads. Plus you should be watchful of your ad's visitor to sales ratio.

148. Order keyword ads from web sites. You could use ad tracking in your paid ads. Also you want to be observant of your ad's target market.

149. Pay for pay per click ads from product directories. You may use good spelling in your paid ads. And you need to be wary of your ad's niche profits.

150. Invest in classified ads from auction web sites. You should use myth statements in your paid ads. Plus you should be alert of your ad's investment returns.

151. Purchase banner ads from forums. You can use your professional picture in your paid ads. Also you want to be overseeing your ad's total cost.

152. Buy sponsor ads from event hosts. You might use endorsements in your paid ads. And you need to be keeping tabs of your ad's value.

153. Order insert ads from product shippers. You could use names in your paid ads. Plus you should be attentive of your ad's bottom line.

154. Pay for outsource ads from freelancing web sites. You may use business name in your paid ads. Also you want to be calculating your ad's watchers to sales ratios.

155. Invest in press releases ads from publicity web sites. You should use success stories in your paid ads. And you need to be alert of your ad's listeners to sales rates.

156. Purchase pop up ads from file sharing webs sites. You can use instructions in your paid ads. Plus you should be keeping track of your ad profit gains.

157. Buy audio ads from teleseminar broadcasters. You might use quantity information in your paid ads. Also you want to be totaling your ad's reader to sales ratios.

158. Order top sponsor ads from search engines. You could use celebrities in your paid ads. And you need to be watchful of your ad's long tern customers.

159. Pay for commercial ad from ad agencies. You may use USP in your paid ads. Plus you should be observant of your ad expenses.

160.   Invest in text link ads from web sites. You should use slogans in your paid ads. Also you want to be wary of your ad fees.

CHAPTER 9

161.   Purchase solo ads from fax companies. You can use bullet points in your paid ads. And you need to be alert of your ad prices.

162.   Buy mobile ads from mobile ad agencies. You might use music in your paid ads. Plus you should be overseeing your ad charges.

163.   Order pay per click ads from news web sites. You could use opt-in forms in your paid ads. Also you want to be keeping tabs of your ad finances.

164.   Pay for audio ads from audio sharing networks. You may use sound effects in your paid ads. And you need to be attentive of your ad's income amount.

165.   Invest in upsells ads from product sellers. You should use countdown counters in your paid ads. Plus you should be calculating your ad's repeat orders.

166. Purchase yellow page ads from online yellow page sites. You can use good grammar in your paid ads. Also you want to be alert of your ad expenditures.

167. Buy pic ads from image sharing sites. You might use logos in your paid ads. And you need to be keeping track of your ad revenue.

168. Order store ads from payment processors. You could use demonstrations in your paid ads. Plus you should be totaling your ad money.

169. Pay for interview ads from magazines. You may use beliefs in your paid ads. Also you want to be watchful of your ad's success.

170. Invest in web site ads from traffic exchange sites. You should use multiple fonts in your paid ads. And you need to be observant of your ad purchases.

171. Purchase viral ads from online freebie publishers. You can use videos in your paid ads. Plus you should be wary of your ad's transactions.

172. Buy insert flyer ads from newspapers. You might use empathy in your paid ads. Also you want to be alert of your ad funds.

173. Order discount ads from coupon companies. You could use ad testing in your paid ads. And you need to be overseeing your ad's savings.

174. Pay for radio ads from radio stations. You may use terms and conditions in your paid ads. Plus you should be keeping tabs of your ad's capital.

175. Invest in banners ads from web directories. You should use secret curiosity in your paid ads. Also you want to be attentive of your ad's tests.

176. Purchase booth ads from trade shows. You can use good punctuation in your paid ads. And you need to be calculating your ad's experiments.

177. Buy content ads from contextual ad companies. You might use tips in your paid ads. Plus you should be alert of your ad's tracking.

178. Order sponsor ads from report publishers. You could use colored text in your paid ads. Also you want to be keeping track of your ad's feedback.

179. Pay for wanted ads from career/job sites. You may use borders in your paid ads. And you need to be totaling your ad kitty.

180. Invest in product review ads from review web sites. You should use personal opinions in your paid ads. Plus you should be watchful of your ad's worth.

CHAPTER 10

181. Purchase app ads from add web sites. You can use free services in your paid ads. Also you want to be observant of your ad changes.

182. Buy banner ads from free web hosting sites. You might use product ratings in your paid ads. And you need to be wary of your ad vestment.

183. Order display ads from stores. You could use samples in your paid ads. Plus you should be alert of your ad funding.

184. Pay for promo product ads from specialty advertising services. You may use emotional words in your paid ads. Also you want to be overseeing your ad cash.

185. Invest in commercial ads from cable stations. You should use product jingles in your paid ads. And you need to be keeping tabs of your ad's modifications.

186. Purchase graphical ads from image sharing web sites. You can use peer pressure in your paid ads. Plus you should be attentive of your ad's account.

187. Buy text link ads from blogs. You might use the word 'free' in your paid ads. Also you want to be calculating your ad's competition.

188. Order background ads from web sites. You could use artwork in your paid ads. And you need to be alert of your ad's impressions.

189. Pay for yellow page ads from phone books. You may use background info in your paid ads. Plus you should be keeping track of your ad's reactions.

190. Invest in comment ads from blogs publishers. You should use positive language in your paid ads. Also you want to be totaling your ad debt.

191. Purchase banner ads from membership web sites. You can use their wants in your paid ads. And you need to be watchful of your ad's click- throughs.

192. Buy keyword/phrase text ads from content web sites. You might use target keywords in your paid ads. Plus you should be observant of your ad's visibility.

193. Order radio ads from online radio stations. You could use Aida formula in your paid ads. Also you want to be wary of your ad's adjustments.

194. Pay for business cards from printer places. You may use colored backgrounds in your paid ads. And you need to be alert of your ad's sign ups.

195. Invest in placement ads from movie/tv producers. You should use product pics/covers in your paid ads. Plus you should be overseeing your ad's placements.

196. Purchase word of mouth from commissioned sales men/woman. You can use professionals for your paid ads. Also you want to be keeping tabs of your ad's marketing.

197. Buy car/vehicle sins ads from transportation services. You might use magnetic signs for your paid ads. And you need to be attentive of your ad's movement.

198. Order branded cross promotion ads from famous businesses. You could use business reputations in your paid ads. Plus you should be calculating your ad's promotions.

199. Pay for paid endorsements ads from famous people. You may use celebrity reputations in your paid ads. Also you want to be alert of your ad's popularity.

200. Invest in preview ads from dvd producers/movie theaters. You should use video presentations in your paid ads. And you need to be keeping track of your ad's previews.

Printed by Libri Plureos GmbH in Hamburg,
Germany